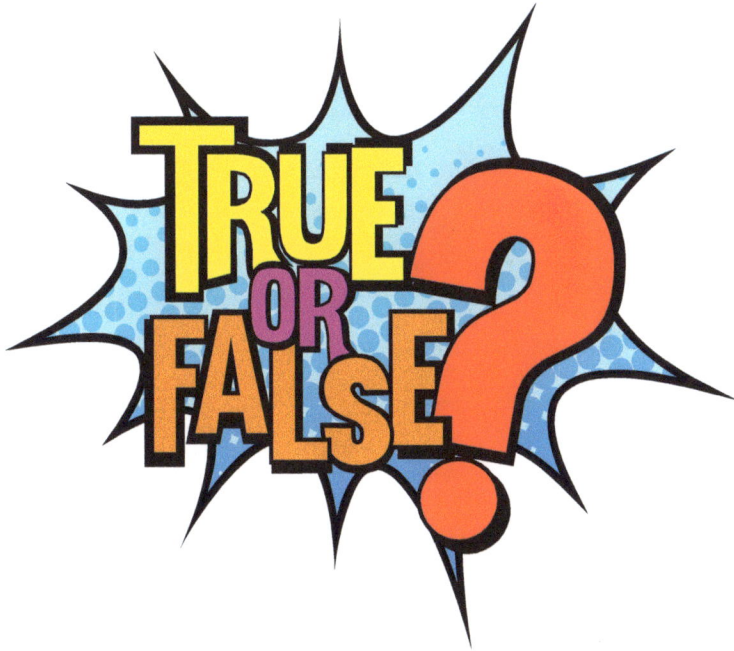

Co-published by agreement between Shi Tu Hui and World Book, Inc.

Shi Tu Hui
Room 1807, Block 1,
#3 West Dawang Road
Chaoyang District, Beijing 100025
P.R. China

World Book, Inc.
180 North LaSalle Street
Suite 900
Chicago, Illinois 60601
USA

Library of Congress Cataloging-in-Publication Data for this volume has been applied for.

True or False? (set #4)
ISBN: 978-0-7166-5417-9 (set, hc.)

Explorers
ISBN: 978-0-7166-5424-7 (hc.)

Also available as:
ISBN: 978-0-7166-5434-6 (e-book)
ISBN: 978-0-7166-5444-5 (soft cover)

Staff

Executive Committee

President
Geoff Broderick

Vice President, Editorial
Tom Evans

Vice President, Finance
Molly Stedron

Vice President, International and Marketing
Eddy Kisman

Vice President, Technology and Operations
Jason Dole

Director, Human Resources
Bev Ecker

Editorial

Writer
Jenna Neely

Manager, New Content
Jeff De La Rosa

Associate Manager, New Content
William D. Adams

Curriculum Designer
Caroline Davidson

Proofreader
Nathalie Strassheim

Graphics and Design

Coordinator, Design Development & Production:
Brenda Tropinski

Senior Visual Communications Designer
Melanie Bender

Senior Media Editor
Rosalia Bledsoe

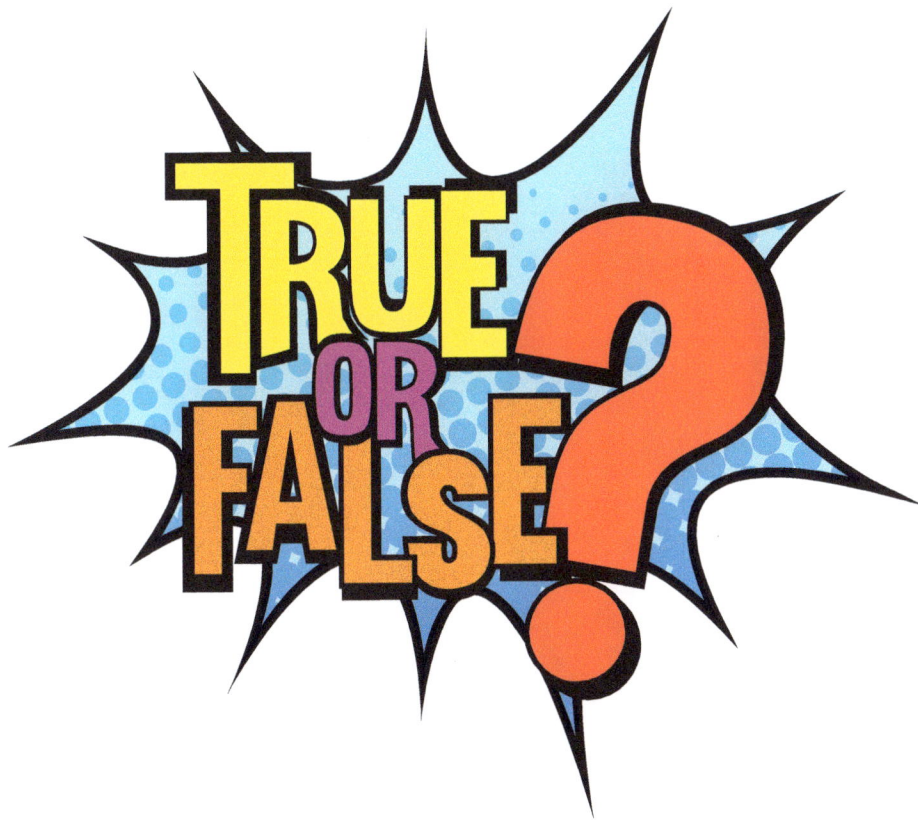

TRUE OR FALSE?

EXPLORERS

WORLD BOOK

www.worldbook.com

TRUE OR FALSE?

The American astronaut Neil Armstrong was the first human to set foot on the moon.

TRUE!

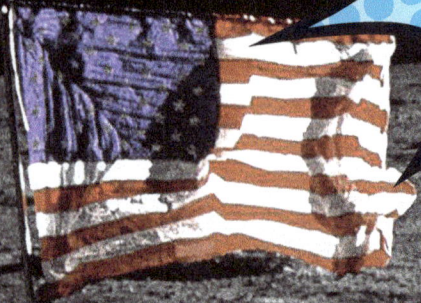

Armstrong's left foot made the first human contact with the moon on July 20, 1969, on the Apollo 11 mission.

As he stepped on the moon, he famously announced,

"That's one small step for a man, one giant leap for mankind."

TRUE OR FALSE?

The explorer Christopher Columbus named America after his younger sister.

9

FALSE!

The Italian merchant Amerigo Vespucci claimed he was the first to discover South America.

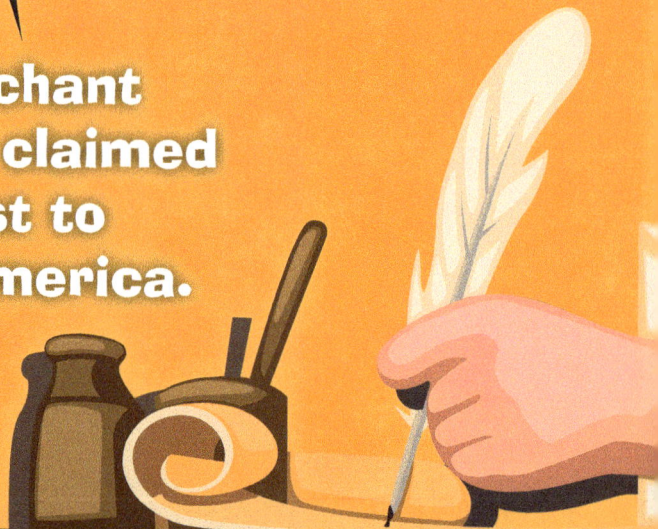

A German *cartographer* (mapmaker) wrote Amerigo's name on a map of the New World, naming the Americas. Columbus did not get the chance to name the country he claimed to discover.

TRUE OR FALSE?

A stray dog from the streets of Moscow is remembered as a pioneer of space travel.

SPUTNIK 2 3. NOVEMBER 1958
LAIKA

13

TRUE!

The dog, later named Laika, was launched into orbit on the craft Sputnik 2 on Nov. 3, 1957. Laika's flight helped pave the way for human travel in space.

SPOUTNIK 1

SPOUTNIK 2

CCCP

TRUE OR FALSE?

The French scientist Jeanne Baret became the first woman to *circumnavigate* (sail all the way around) the world in the 1770's.

TRUE!

The young Frenchwoman disguised herself as a male servant to one of the scientists on the expedition. The trick worked until the expedition reached the Polynesian island of Tahiti. The Tahitians quickly realized that Baret was a woman.

TRUE OR FALSE?

The ship *Endurance* disappeared forever after carrying the British explorer Ernest Shackleton and his crew to Antarctica in 1914.

LIEUT. E. H. SHACKLETON

Shackleton and his crew did have to abandon the ship, which became trapped in sea ice and finally sank. But, it was not lost forever. In 2022, searchers discovered the wreck of the *Endurance* at the bottom of the Weddell Sea, east of the Antarctic Peninsula. It was about 4 miles (6 kilometers) from the ship's last recorded position.

TRUE OR FALSE?

The goal of the Lewis and Clark expedition was to find gold on the western frontier of North America.

FALSE!

The goal of the expedition was to explore the newly purchased Louisiana Territory. In addition, the explorers wanted to meet *Indigenous* (native) peoples. They were also looking for a sea passage from the Atlantic Ocean to the Pacific.

The United States government sponsored the expedition, led by Army officers Meriwether Lewis and William Clark. President Thomas Jefferson considered the mission a success, and that is almost as good as gold!

28

TRUE OR FALSE?

The Soviet Union was the first nation to reach space, kicking off the Space Age.

TRUE!

The Space Age began on Oct. 4, 1957, when the Soviet Union launched Sputnik, the first artificial satellite to *orbit* (circle) Earth. (The Soviet Union was a Communist country that included Russia and parts of other present-day countries.)

TRUE OR FALSE?

The Buddhist monk Xuanzang, one of China's most famous explorers, traveled more than 10,000 miles (16,000 kilometers) by foot and horse.

TRUE!

In the early 600's, Xuanzang traveled to India and other countries to collect Buddhist scriptures and learn about Buddhism from other scholars. His incredible journey took over 16 years.

TRUE OR FALSE?

An interest in hang gliding led the Soviet cosmonaut Valentina Tereshkova to become the first woman in space.

FALSE!

Tereshkova's hobby was parachuting. She made more than 125 jumps before volunteering for spaceflight training. Tereshkova became the first woman in space when she orbited Earth 48 times aboard the craft Vostok 6 in 1963.

TRUE OR FALSE?

A version of the web browser Internet Explorer was developed under the code name Rincón, a popular surfing beach in Puerto Rico.

Microsoft began naming internet products after surf locations because people use them to "surf" the internet! Rincón is the Caribbean's surfing capital. It is also home to many humpback whales and an ideal place to explore.

TRUE OR FALSE?

The Portuguese sea captain Ferdinand Magellan became the first person to sail around the world.

FALSE!

Magellan set out to sail around the world in 1519. But, only one ship in his fleet, the *Victoria,* made it back to Spain to complete the trip. Magellan himself died in a battle among rival groups on the Philippine island of Mactan.

TRUE OR FALSE?

The farthest a human
has traveled from
Earth is to the planet
Venus.

49

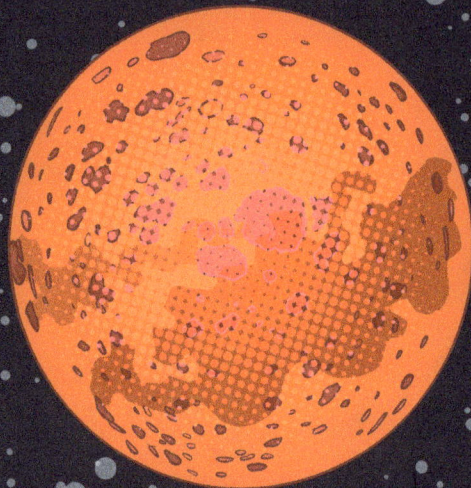

Humans have only ventured a little past the moon and back. The Apollo 13 mission traveled the farthest, reaching almost 250,000 miles (400,000 kilometers) away. To get to Venus, astronauts would have to travel more than 500 times farther!

TO VENUS

TRUE OR FALSE?

One of the earliest known exploratory expeditions was *commissioned* (ordered) by a woman.

Queen Hatshepsut of Egypt sent an expedition by way of the Red Sea to the land of Punt in the 1400's B.C. The exact location of Punt is not known. It may have been in southwest Arabia or the Somali coast of Africa.

TRUE OR FALSE?

The Bering Strait was named for all the bears that like to fish there.

FALSE!

The Bering Strait is named after the Danish explorer Vitus Bering. It is a narrow stretch of water that separates Alaska and Russia. Bering was working for Russia when he crossed the strait to sight Alaska in 1741. Bering's voyages led Russia to claim Alaska. (Russia later sold Alaska to the United States.)

TRUE OR FALSE?

The New Zealand mountain climber Sir Edmund Hillary reached the summit of Mount Everest on his first climb of the mountain.

The third time was the charm. Hillary climbed Everest part of the way in 1951 and again in 1952. On his third expedition, he and Tenzing Norgay, a Sherpa guide from Nepal, reached the summit on May 29, 1953. They became the first two men to reach the top of Mount Everest and return.

THE TIMES
EVEREST
COLOUR SUPPLEMENT
1953
LONDON   PRICE 3s. 6d.

COMPANIONS IN ACHIEVEMENT
Sir Edmund Hillary and Tenzing Norkey, G.M., who together climbed Everest on Friday, May 29, 1953.

Volume CCXIII   No. 2785   The SPHERE, London, June 27, 1953
The SPHERE
with which is incorporated THE GRAPHIC

TRUE OR FALSE?

The Norse explorer Leif Eriksson was the first European to reach North America, nearly 500 years before Columbus reached the New World.

65

TRUE!

Eriksson led what was probably the first European expedition to the mainland of North America around 1000 A.D. Historians do not know where he landed. But it was probably in what is now Newfoundland, Canada.

TRUE OR FALSE?

Marco Polo invented a popular swimming game similar to playing tag with closed eyes.

FALSE!

Marco Polo was a Venetian trader who traveled to central Asia and China in the 1300's. He was not the first European to reach China. But, he wrote a book that introduced many Europeans to the country. Historians have not been able to connect Marco Polo to any swimming games.

TRUE OR FALSE?

A newspaper sent the journalist Henry Morgan Stanley to find the explorer David Livingstone when he was lost in Africa.

DAILY NEWS

EXTRA!
EXTRA!

73

The Scottish explorer David Livingstone captured the public's imagination by writing about Africa. But, he disappeared there in the late 1860's. In 1869, the *New York Herald* newspaper sent Stanley to find him. Stanley found Livingstone at Lake Tanganyika, in east-central Africa, in early November 1871. Stanley greeted him with the now-famous words: "Dr. Livingstone, I presume?"

David Livingstone

Henry Morgan Stanley

TRUE OR FALSE?

The Black pioneer Jean Baptiste Point Du Sable discovered the five Great Lakes.

FALSE!

Du Sable traveled from Haiti to what is now the Chicago area and established a trading post. His farm was near Lake Michigan, but he did not discover the Great Lakes.

Two men raced to become the first to reach the South Pole, but only one survived

TRUE!

The British explorer Robert Falcon Scott and the Norwegian explorer Roald Amundsen both set out to be the first to reach the South Pole in 1910.

Amundsen and his men reached the South Pole on Dec. 14, 1911. Scott's crew reached the South Pole five weeks later, only to find that Amundsen had beaten them. All five men in Scott's crew died on the return trip.

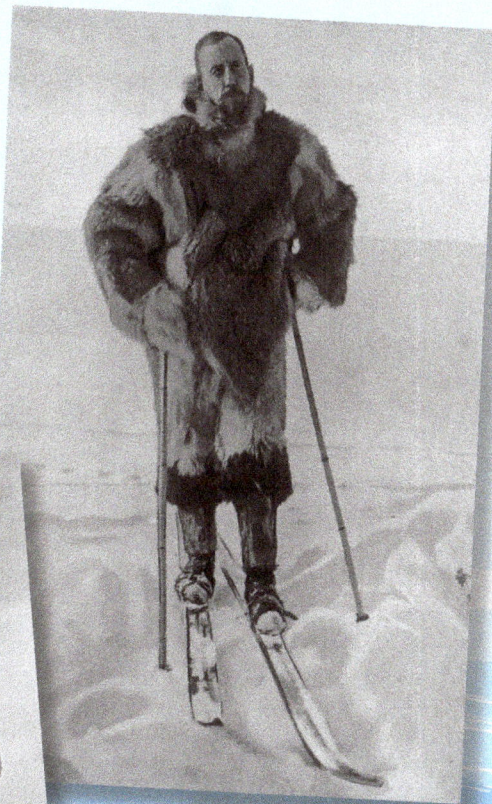

Roald Amundsen

Robert Falcon Scott

TRUE OR FALSE?

The first woman to walk in space also became the first to reach the deepest point in the oceans.

In 1984, the United States astronaut Kathryn Sullivan became the first woman to walk in space, during a mission aboard the space shuttle Challenger. In 2020, Sullivan became the first woman to reach Challenger Deep in the Pacific Ocean, the deepest known point on Earth. Sullivan seems to be the real challenger. How many more records can she set?

EYOS
EXPEDITIONS

TRITON

TRUE OR FALSE?

The Black explorer Matthew Henson coined the phrase "finders keepers" after discovering the North Pole.

FALSE!

No one knows who coined the term. However, Henson served on the American explorer Robert Peary's expedition to reach the North Pole.

Some historians believe that Henson and two Inuit were the first to reach the pole. But Peary got credit for the discovery— going down in history as the finder and the keeper!

DID YOU KNOW...

According to popular legend, the Spanish explorer Ponce de León came to Florida to find the **Fountain of Youth.** But he was actually interested in finding wealth and conquering new lands.

The word *explore* was first used as a hunting term and means *cry out.* Hunters would shout to see if game was in a hunting area.

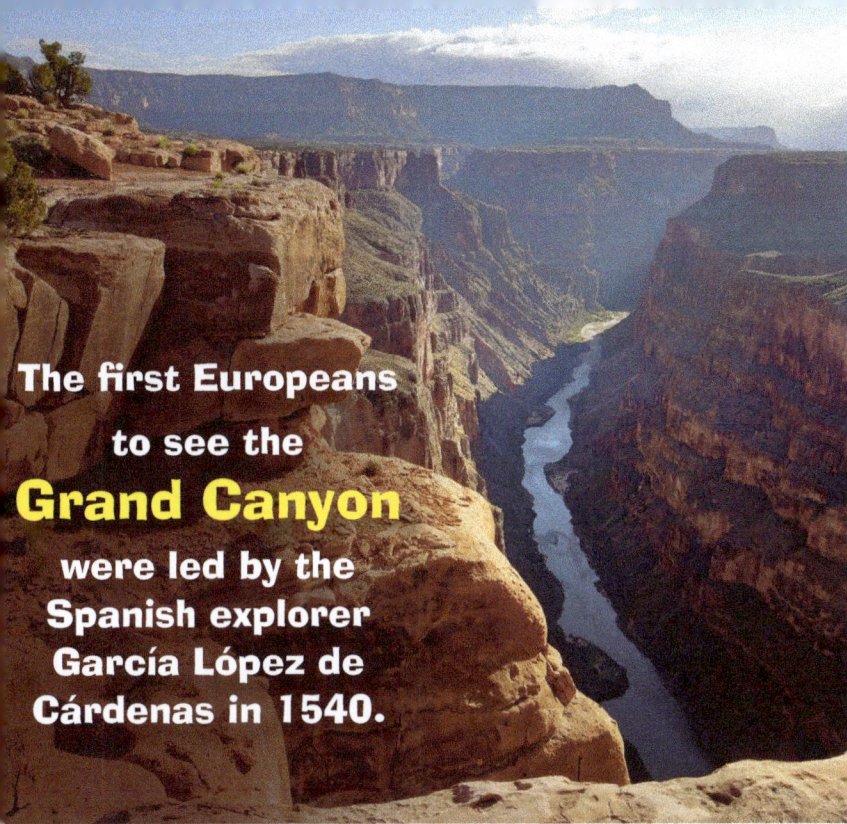

The first Europeans to see the **Grand Canyon** were led by the Spanish explorer García López de Cárdenas in 1540.

The American explorer Sylvia Earle set the record for the **deepest untethered solo dive** when she walked on the floor of the Pacific Ocean 1,250 feet (380 meters) below the surface.

Sailors in the 1700's believed bananas were **bad luck** on boats. The superstition is still widely held today.

ENGAGE YOUR READER

GUIDED READING PROMPTS

Before Reading

- Allow readers to scan the text and discuss what they notice so far. Highlight the structure of this text and explain that the answers include both evidence and reasoning that support the claim of true or false.
- Explain the literacy skill: *Sometimes authors write a claim and then use evidence and reasoning to help make their point clear. Look for these elements as you read!*

During Reading

- Read each statement and provide time to discuss whether readers believe it to be true or false before turning the page to learn the facts.
- As you read, model how to identify the claims, evidence, and reasoning in the text. Prompt your readers to identify these features as they explore the text, too.
- Encourage readers to further discuss their learning by pausing to discuss surprising information.

After Reading

- Prompt your readers to connect, extend, and challenge their thinking about the text:
  - What will you take away from reading this text?
  - What changes in your thinking happened while reading and learning?
  - What is still challenging your thinking? What questions or wonderings do you still have?

LOOK BACK!

- Prompt readers to look back through the text to identify examples of interesting or thought-provoking claims.
- Challenge readers to explain what makes these examples so engaging.

CURRICULUM CONNECTIONS

These questions and tasks support the following English/Language Arts skills:

- Determining what a text says both explicitly and implicitly
- Citing specific evidence when drawing conclusions
- Interpreting words and phrases used in a text
- Analyzing how the structure of a text affects how it is read.

LITERACY SKILL

Authors make their claims stronger by supporting them with evidence and reasoning.

- A claim is a statement of truth.
- Evidence includes the facts or information that prove whether the claim is true.
- Reasoning includes any logical explanation that describes how the evidence supports the claim.

Example from the text: Pages 24-27

- Claim: The goal of the Lewis and Clark expedition was *not* to find gold.
- Evidence: The goal was to explore new land, meet Indigenous people, and find a waterway between the Pacific and Atlantic Oceans.
- Reasoning: The US government had just purchased the large Louisiana Territory and wanted to know more about it.

EXTEND THROUGH WRITING

Challenge readers to create their own True/False questions and answers about explorers.

- Have readers use a trusted reference, such as www.worldbookonline.com, to research information related to explorers. Encourage readers to look for key details, fun facts, or surprising features that would make strong True or False statements.
- Give readers one notecard for each claim they research.
- Direct readers to write the claim on the front of the notecard. On the back, readers should describe why that claim is true or false using evidence and reasoning from their research.

MORE WAYS TO ENGAGE!

- Play a game! After considering each claim, have readers signify "true" with a thumb up and "false" with a thumb down. Keep score to see who knows their facts about explorers the best!
  - Develop collaboration skills by grouping readers together into teams.
- Further discuss any True/False claims that revealed readers' misconceptions. Focus the conversation on *why* they initially thought what they did and how the text helped them learn.

Acknowledgments

Cover © Benchart/Shutterstock;
© Sergiy Bykhunenko, Shutterstock;
© Vector Pixel Star/Shutterstock;
© Frozenbunn/Shutterstock

4-5 © Mr. Somchat Parkaythong, Shutterstock
6-7 NASA
8-11 © Shutterstock
12-13 © World History Archive/Alamy Images
14-15 © Alexander Mitrofanov, Alamy Images
16-17 © Enrique Alaez Perez, Shutterstock
18-23 Public Domain
24-25 © agefotostock/Alamy Images
27-31 © Shutterstock
32-33 © Imaginechina Limited/Alamy Images
34-35 © CPA Media Pte Ltd/Alamy Images
36-37 © Mny-Jhee, Shutterstock
38-39 © Sergey Ginak, Shutterstock; © Pictorial Press Ltd/Alamy Images
40-43 © Shutterstock
44-45 © Universal Art Archive/Alamy Images
46-47 © Prisma Archivo/Alamy Images
48-53 © Shutterstock
54-55 © Jenny Lipets, Shutterstock; © Chronicle/Alamy Images
56-57 © Sonsedska Yuliia, Shutterstock
58-59 © Album/Alamy Images
60-61 © Vixit/Shutterstock
62-63 © Vixit/Shutterstock; © The Times; © Chronicle/Alamy Images
64-65 © PA Images/Alamy Images
66-67 Leif Eriksson Discovers America, oil on canvas by Hans Dahl (Public Domain)
68-69 © BNP Design Studio/Shutterstock
70-71 © Naci Yavuz (fogbird), Alamy Images
72-73 © Art Puppy/iStock
74-75 © Tatsiana Hendzel, Shutterstock; © Tomnamon/Shutterstock; © Colport/Alamy Images
76-77 © DeLoyd Huenink, Shutterstock
78-79 © JaySi/Shutterstock; USPS
80-81 © Shutterstock
82-83 © Shutterstock; © Classic Image/Alamy Images; Public Domain
84-85 NASA
86-87 © Caladan Oceanic LLC.
88-89 © Kris Grabiec, Shutterstock; Public Domain
90-91 © Universal Art Archive/Alamy Images
92-94 © Shutterstock

www.ingramcontent.com/pod-product-compliance
Lightning Source LLC
Chambersburg PA
CBHW061408090426
42740CB00023B/3473